FEARS, FOCUS, AND

MENTAL FREEDOM.

The Tools Are Here.

Are you terrified of trying that new skill? Have you lost the joy of gymnastics? Have you felt pressure to perform as a gymnast, even when you don't believe in yourself?

In this practical, easy to understand and action-oriented book, Amy Twiggs, Director of Flippin' Awesome Gymnastics, will help you apply proven methods to overcome self-doubt. Twiggs has personally used every piece of information in this book herself for many years in her successful career.

You will remember you're good enough, strong enough, and brave enough to attempt skills you once thought impossible in gymnastics.

Twiggs explains, "As a former competitive gymnast, I've been there; I know what it feels like to try your best and to fail. I also know how it feels to work hard to achieve your goals. I know the feelings of being terrified of a new skill, losing the joy of gymnastics, and having a desire to quit."

Flippin' Awesome Gymnast, Vol. I reveals a proven approach designed to resolve your struggles with insecurities and frustrations in the gym.

In this how-to guide, you'll be given tools to:

- Keep you motivated as a gymnast
- Stay focused as you reach your peak performance
- Achieve your highest potential
- Enjoy the journey of the sport

No matter your current level of ability, this book provides proven strategies to overcome limiting beliefs that affect your score. It addresses self-confidence and high performance issues that will help you **crush your fears and increase confidence.**

Don't let your time as a gymnast keep slipping away-- take it back, make it productive, and enjoy your new gymnastics life.

Our thoughts are always ours to choose. **Elite gymnasts choose power.**

Making no change to your daily gymnastics routine is like living in your past presently. It's time to pass Level 1. **3-2-1 Go!**

FLIPPIN' AWESOME GYMNAST

VOL. I

**5 Tools to Crush Fear &
Increase Confidence
for Gymnasts**

Amy Twiggs

ISBN-13: 978-1-949015-00-3

TABLE OF CONTENTS

Dedication

I would like to dedicate this book to the following people:

—MY PARENTS
They have always been my greatest fans. Their dedication to my personal and athletic success continues to inspire me. I'm continually grateful for their guidance and unconditional love.

—MY HUSBAND, TYLER
He has supported my efforts to strive to become someone better than I was yesterday. His patience and sacrifice on my behalf is endearing and appreciated.

—FOUR WONDERFUL TEENAGERS
Every day, I get to learn from my teenagers. They are each unique. However, together, they make an entertaining and dynamic team. Much of my joy comes from being near these amazing youths. Every gymnast, coach and team I have had the pleasure of working with, thank you!

AND ALL OF YOU WHO ARE READING THIS BOOK
-THANK YOU-

INTRODUCTION

For a gymnast, there's an unspoken rule of compliant behavior in hopes of obtaining a perfect 10.0 someday. As your workouts become increasingly more difficult, you may find that you feel mentally stuck, incapable of moving forward, constant anxiety, or a loss of passion for gymnastics.

This book helps you remember your first love: gymnastics. You'll recall the reasons you felt you were good enough, strong enough, and brave enough to attempt skills you once thought impossible. The *Flippin' Awesome Gymnast* book has been designed to resolve your struggles with insecurities and frustrations in the gym. This book provides strategies to overcome limiting beliefs that affect your score. It's also for gymnasts who struggle with fears and self-confidence.

As a former competitive gymnast, I want you to know that I've been there. I know what it feels like to try your best and to fail over and over. I know what it feels like to work hard to achieve your goals. I understand the feelings of being terrified of a new skill, losing the joy of gymnastics, and having a desire to quit.

Gymnasts and others who suffer from emotional insecurities and mental blocks have experienced great success by utilizing the methods found in this helpful guide to crush fears and increase confidence.

Elaina, a gymnast at Coral Peak Gymnastics in Utah says, "The best thing about this book is it is short and powerful. I have used these tools and instantly felt a lot more confident in the gym. They work!"

I promise if you implement the five simple tools found in this book, you'll immediately see and feel increased excitement for gymnastics again, have more desire to overcome fears, and feel peaceful and calm instead of anxious when moments are tough. Don't be the person who misses out on this opportunity in your athletic life because you tried to push through your trials and fears on your own.

Be the person others look to for inspiration. Be the kind of person others look at and wonder, *How do they do that?* Be the kind of person who takes some action right now to make a change in their life today.

The quick tools you're about to learn have been used by many to create positive and enduring results. All you have to do is use the tips one at a time, keep reading, and begin to apply the new strategies today. Each chapter will give you a new tool to become the gymnast you've always dreamed of becoming. Decide now to take another step toward a higher level of gymnastic performance than you've ever imagined. 3-2-1, Go!

My Story:

"Don't be afraid if things seem difficult in the beginning. That's only the initial impression. The important thing is not to retreat; you have to master yourself."

—Olga Korbut, gold medal gymnast

"There's no situation that will ever have power over you if you know who you are. Knowing who you are will change what you want. Knowing what you want will change what you believe. Knowing what you believe creates a future of limitless possibilities!"

—Amy Twiggs

My elite routine began to develop when I was in kindergarten. I started gymnastics at the age of eight. Whether I was at the gym or watching the Olympics, I found myself intently observing higher-level gymnasts perform tricks that looked exhilarating. I was constantly imagining myself doing those same skills. Gymnastics became a part of my soul. It was woven into the fabric of my life. There was no separating gymnastics from me.

Just like any enthusiastic young gymnast, you would find me doing handstands and practicing the next skill outside our home on the grass or on the metal bars at my elementary school after the last bell rang. I recall ripping off a large part of the skin on my palm in the process of learning skills on those metal bars. What was a little flesh wound in exchange for feeling the rhythm of a bar kip as I would pop my body up onto the bar?

(A bar kip is a movement on the uneven parallel bars in which you glide your body under the bar, extend fully, and then pull yourself to a resting position with your stomach on the bar.)

In 3rd grade, I recall an elderly teacher with red curly hair who saw me working aerials, a maneuver in which you perform a cartwheel with no hands touching the ground. I was using the edge of the sidewalk outside this teacher's classroom door to practice. Instead of telling me to stop, she encouraged me to keep trying. I executed my first true aerial in front of that teacher and received an applause to boot.

At that time in my gymnastics career, I knew nothing about the importance of nutrition, sleep, and mental toughness; I just knew that I enjoyed flipping.

By the age of 15, I had progressed considerably as a gymnast. The Junior Olympics, or J.O., gymnastics program starts at level 1, progresses to level 10, and ends at Elite as the highest level. Level 10 and Elite gymnasts compete at college or in the Olympics. Typically, a competitive gymnast begins at level 3 then works through each level until they qualify for Elite.

During my club gymnastics years, I trained with the Arizona Twisters. At that time, Arizona Twisters didn't compete at level 10. Instead, the gymnasts would try out for elite after level 9. This was a legal and common path for many higher-level gymnasts at that time. I had attended two Elite qualification meets with two teammates, both of whom had reached the qualifying score on their first try, but I had not. They still came to the other qualifying meets just for more experience.

I didn't know it at the time, but my parents had purchased a necklace for me with my name and the word "elite" engraved on it, which they planned to give to me after the first qualifying meet. When I did finally qualify for elite after the third meet, my parents presented me with the necklace and I inquired about it. My dad told me he and my mom both knew I would become an elite eventually; there was no question in their minds. They knew it just like I did.

Failing at my first two attempts didn't discourage me from working a little harder to make my routines just a little better in order to progress further in the sport. This is the nature of gymnastics.

I currently love the song, "Get Back Up Again" from the movie, Trolls. To me, this is the perfect theme song for a gymnast's life. Every day, we fall in practice over and over, but we learn from day one of gymnastics that you always get back up again. There's no holding a gymnast down for long. Lingering in self-pity on the ground doesn't serve any gymnast well.

Around this same age, I was taught positive affirmations and visualization techniques by my older brother during the summer he spent home from college. These tools, along with relaxation and breathing techniques, became a consistent part of my daily routine. I attribute much of my confidence and success as an elite gymnast to those four tools.

At the age of 16, I experienced a kind of out-of-body episode because I had practiced visualization in such detail every night before I fell asleep. At that time, I was preparing for a national team qualifying competition that was to take place at the Delta Center in Salt Lake City, Utah.

For six months prior to that competition, I had daily visualized the eight routines I was to perform. One tumbling pass, in particular, had caused me some anxiety in practice, but no longer held any power over me due to the visualization technique. Upon landing that tumbling pass at the competition, I experienced dèjá vu in a way I had never before felt it. The details of my routines were all performed precisely as I had envisioned them to be.

Although I had never actually been in the Delta Center, the arena layout, equipment set up, and general audience were everything I had imagined in my mind they would be. For a brief moment, I wasn't sure if I was in my bed at home visualizing this pass or actually performing at the arena.

Instantly, I knew there was power in the thoughts I had created in my mind and the words I had chosen to believe. It was beyond my ability to clearly explain. Since that experience at the Delta Center, I have used those same tools to adapt and refine my daily routine to become the person I am today.

I obtained a full-ride women's gymnastics scholarship and received a Psychology Degree from Stanford University. I am now a wife to an amazing man and a mother of four teenagers. I also own a gymnastics company, Flippin' Awesome Gymnastics, where I love to continually serve gymnasts.

My daily routine from the age of 15 to the present and in the future will continue to progress as I learn, understand, and gain more knowledge and life experience.

High-performing athletes often hear comments such as, "I don't know how you do all you do" or "Why do you want to do all that?" or "You should just sit and relax more often" or "I could never do what you do." Many people are astonished by the intense regimens that elite athletes choose.

Anyone can live an elite lifestyle if they choose to. Motive and desire are keys to any change. If you're reading this book, then chances are you have a desire to make changes to your current athletic routine.

I am offering athletic techniques that are applicable to everyone. If utilized, these tools will get you to a more impactful level of daily performance. This book will inspire greatness, increase confidence, and crush fears.

When you create your moments, days, dreams, and life, you're living intentionally. Do those hard things, make those uncomfortable choices, surprise yourself by exposing your own undiscovered capabilities. Elite performers narrow their daily choices to produce unimaginable results.

1

Blast Off

Sequence

"If not now, then when?"

—John E. Lewis

"Gold medals aren't really made of gold. They're made of sweat, determination, and a hard-to-find alloy called guts."

—Dan Gable

"She believed she could, so she did."

—R. S. Grey

CHAPTER 1 TOOLS:

THE BLAST OFF SEQUENCE

The blast off sequence is the mental and physical tool to get you moving without hesitation. If you know there's no logical reason not to move forward, then you make the decision about or take action on something, without hesitation.

Count backwards to yourself out loud, "3-2-1 Go!" and then move toward that goal without hesitating. If you hesitate, immediately take a step back from the goal. Make a new, improved, and more doable plan.

Work your way up to mentally, physically, and emotionally move "without hesitation" at the higher level. The purpose of this tool is to teach you how to make yourself get up and move because if you hesitate in life, then whatever you want to happen, probably won't.

You don't need to know how something will unfold, you just need to *be willing* and then start moving.

~

Gymnasts get the opportunity to refine themselves daily through constantly fine-tuning every aspect of their gymnastics life. This is easy for a gymnast to understand when relating to the beam. Gymnasts know they'll fall off the beam.

In fact, they're never surprised at a fall when beginning to learn a skill on the beam. It's expected. As much as they don't want to fall, they're absolutely aware of the fact that it's simply part of the process of learning a new skill.

If a gymnast falls and stays down, their progression of the sport is done. They won't become an elite. Gymnasts learn this very quickly and naturally. When watching a gymnast workout, you'll notice that if a gymnast falls, they almost always bounce back on the beam.

They are continually self-correcting or listening to a coach correct any mistakes. It takes a while, sometimes, to figure out what is "off" on a skill. Are the hips square, is the rhythm off, are the shoulders even, is the lift strong, are they pushing through their toes, or is something else going on mentally?

After hours, days, weeks, and years of hard work, they get to enjoy climbing up on that beam, do breathing techniques, mental checks, cue words (words they will repeat vocally to keep their mind focused on something that increases their level of success on that skill), and any other emotional, mental, and physical preparation routine they've produced in order to stick ten perfect series in a row.

This is my favorite kind of self-mastery and the closest understanding of how perfection in one small area feels. The satisfaction of doing the hard work required for that experience is all worth the effort to get to that point. However, oftentimes, a gymnast will master a skill only to come to work out the next day and freeze up, balk, or allow fear to take over their body.

What happened? Why can't they force their body to follow through with the skill? How do they make themselves do something when their brain blocks their success?

At times, gymnasts will count backwards, "3,2,1 GO!" when attempting a skill that brings a little added fear or anxiety, even though they usually know logically they *can* physically perform the skill. As a coach of gymnasts for over 25 years, I've had to often stand on stacked panel mats at the side of a beam, waiting for a gymnast to decide whether or not to attempt a new skill or trick.

Coaches use a variety of motivational strategies to summon athletes to go for something they both know the athlete is physically capable of doing. Yet, athletes repeatedly hesitate. The more a gymnast hesitates, the more their body responds to the often-unconscious justifications occurring inside their mind.

This cognitive dissonance or mental debate gains momentum after the first three seconds in any attempt. I've found that the gymnast who hesitates to attempt the trick or skill in the first 1-3 seconds will not attempt it. Eventually, a gymnast may or may not make the effort.

However, those *first few seconds are critical in both the confidence level the gymnast will have in themselves and the level the coach will have in the gymnast.* Because coaches know that there are safety issues when a gymnast hesitates, they cannot allow hesitation to become a habit.

The gymnast is developing mental grooves in the brain. These grooves or neurological pathways work like muscle memory. A response gets easier to repeat the more they entertain it. Once a gymnast hesitates on a skill, the likelihood they will hesitate again goes up exponentially.

A gymnast may unconsciously decide that they're not safe doing the skill or trick on that first attempt, so why not stop again the next time. The gymnast may not be cognizant of these mental games, but it's so easy to recognize the red flags now that I've been a coach, judge, and gym owner for years.

Heart rate increases, feet and hands get sweaty, shoulders tense, and focus is gone. The Mind Guard (discussed in Chapter 4) has been taken down; the gates are wide open for any thought to enter and divert attention.

When a gymnast takes more than three seconds to move on a skill, I ask the gymnast to stop, jump off the beam, take a step down, and decide what they will do on the lower level before attempting a try at the higher level again. They must "do" something successful at a mentally easier level before I'll be willing to spot that gymnast again on a high beam or any level beam they're not quite ready for.

They lose the opportunity to work with me for a time. They must make a cue word and perform a certain number of repetitions of that skill perfectly on a lower level. Once they've successfully completed these terms, then I'll be there for them at the higher level. They get another try.

Either the gymnast or I count out loud, or I count in my head, "3-2-1 Go!" If that moment passes, they must stop and repeat the process in order to receive help from me another time. If a gymnast asks me to spot, and I agree, then I forewarn the gymnast that they will need to go for the skill in 3 seconds; otherwise, they have to move to a more basic area for that skill.

For example, suppose I'm spotting a gymnast on a flic flic lay. This is an advanced move in which a gymnast stands at the very edge of a beam, completes two back handsprings in a row, immediately goes into a stretched backwards flip, landing on the edge of the opposite end of the beam.

If the gymnast stands for over 3 seconds preparing to make their body begin this series, I say, "Your time is up. Go to the low beam and stick 10 flic flic lays (or any beam series), tell me a word (cue word) that helped you at that level, then come back to me when you're done, and I'll be ready to spot you again." I don't allow the gymnast to play around with this choice.

Hesitation involves uncertainty resulting in an act of pausing before a commitment. There's a fine line where a gymnast chooses to go for something or not. If a gymnast is mentally prepared and physically prepared, there's no hesitation. If a gymnast is physically prepared but not mentally prepared, they hesitate, and their justifications and fears take over immediately.

A coach can usually tell as soon as a gymnast walks up to prep for a skill if they're actually going to go for it. If a gymnast is physically and mentally unprepared, then that's just an accident waiting to happen.

This is the "3-2-1 Go!" Rule. Trust is a huge component of gymnastics. If an athlete doesn't know you or trust you, it's difficult to get that athlete to do much at all. When an athlete hesitates on a skill attempt, not only are there safety issues but also the mental games that follow and intensify quickly.

I recall asking a Stanford teammate, Amy Murakami, to do 30 push-ups every time I didn't throw my Tkachev, which is a release on the high uneven bar. It's beyond me why my teammate would agree to this madness. After watching her doing 60 push-ups on my behalf, I gave up on that type of motivation for myself.

Athletes, especially gymnasts, create ways to make their minds do what they know their bodies are capable of performing. Punishing another teammate for my lack of mental strength didn't help either one of us. Well, I guess it helped Amy get a little stronger. The guilt card I tried to play over my mind didn't work. The 3-2-1 card does work, at least, more effectively than doing a skill out of a guilty conscience.

When you feel a strong emotion to try something, then you have two choices: You can respond either positively or negatively to the thought. Those are the choices. Either you grow as a person or diminish. It's that simple.

From my athletic experience, I now believe this life hesitation happens in every area within just a few seconds. What if you applied the "3-2-1 Go!" Rule to every part of our athletic day: when you'll wake up, what foods you'll eat, how you'll think to prepare you for your workout?

After three seconds, you have decided and justified either choice you make. Thoughts will start to build in your mind that hold you back from acting such as "I'm not good enough," "I hope the coach spots really well this time," "My feet are a little slippery," "The bars don't feel right," or "What if I fall?" The feeling to *move* or do some good is fleeting.

However, the feeling to remain stagnant is persistent and dominating. Making a change in your life takes courage. Going for skills or improving your athletic daily routine requires a quick response to those fleeting, inspirational thoughts throughout your day.

By regularly telling yourself, "3-2-1 Go!" in any circumstance, you'll find, more often than not, that you've accomplished something great. You may find that your capabilities astonish even you because you acted with intentional awareness. Try it, 3-2-1 Go!

Chapter 1 Highlights

- Stop wasting time, energy, and endangering your own safety due to indecisiveness during practice.

- The Blast Off Sequence is the mental and physical tool to get you moving without hesitation.

- This easy tool requires you to count backwards, then take action before your brain has time to debate.

- Say out loud, "3-2-1 Go!" to remind your brain what your body already knows how to do it.

- If you hesitate, take a step down mentally or physically. Then build back up to the higher level when you're fully prepared to execute.

What's Ahead in Chapter 2

Learn the method that will create new neurological pathways in your brain in order to have overflowing confidence.

Chapter 1 Action Items

Challenge:

Start each morning by blasting yourself out of bed with the "3-2-1 Go!" Rule, then see how often you can apply it throughout your elite-level day and workouts.

Journal:

Write down one skill that you made yourself do because you told yourself "3-2-1 Go!" before you let you mind persuade you to do otherwise.

If you hesitate to take action, then take time to write down why. Was there really a good reason to hesitate? What might have happened if you had not hesitated?

What's the worst-case scenario? What's the best-case scenario? What might happen in the future if you choose to just go and do, instead of stopping to consider?

2

Brain Game

"The only one who can tell you 'you can't' is you. And you don't have to listen."

—Nike

"Change your thoughts, change your world."

—Author Unknown

CHAPTER 2 TOOLS:

The Brain Game:

The game we play consistently with our thoughts to make our mind believe what we want it to, whether or not it's our current reality. Positive affirmations are statements that we tell ourselves in order to make our thoughts a reality. We create these statements to change our neurological pathways in order to obtain improved results in our performance.

When I was 16, I had thoughts of quitting gymnastics because of hard skills that brought fear, social activities I was missing, and other nonsense I created to justify why gymnastics wasn't the sport for me any longer. My club coach, Lisa Spini, currently USA Master of Sport & International Elite Coach, met with me in her office and asked me what I was going to do if I did quit.

She reminded me of the sacrifice my family had made on my behalf, of the years I had worked to become an elite, and of the future I still possibly had for a college scholarship. I hadn't truly considered what I would do without gymnastics, and the first thing I could think in response to her questions was, "I'll get a scholarship for the oboe!" Lisa looked a little concerned at my sudden decision.

Who was I kidding? Sure, I could play the oboe in band and orchestra, but I didn't love that instrument enough to practice more than the minimal requirement to remain in the high school groups.

Later that evening, my dad took a different approach. He encouraged me to give it "just two more weeks." If I didn't find my love for the sport again in those two weeks, then maybe it was time for me to quit. I agreed to this, and my perspective changed in that short time.

I mastered a couple more skills, gained more courage on old tricks, and the spark was reignited. It had never gone out; I had just chosen to tell myself I didn't like it in my attempts to consider other lifestyles. Ultimately, it was only my thoughts that changed. Nothing else.

Our brain is wired to protect us and only respond in a way that is safe and comfortable. We are the only species that can create false realities. Other species only responds to stimuli when there's an actual threat.

We choose to create these threats, mentally, just in case something happens. We worry about a future that hasn't even occurred. Worry is not a present thought.

We create scenarios that might happen instead of dealing with situations that actually are happening. We want great change coupled with mental and emotional safety.

However, change doesn't always come in a comfortable environment. We must be willing to FEEL uncomfortable mentally, physically, and emotionally if we want any great change in our lives. Fear is a part of life. *If we choose to remain the same, then we are choosing to live in our past presently.*

The positive affirmation tool is one in which you're going to be telling yourself ideas that you don't currently fully believe are in your life. These words will create new neurological pathways in your brain, but only if you're consistent and have a desire to believe what you tell yourself.

An affirmation is a statement of who you are, not who you're going to become. That's the basic power of The Brain Game exercise. You're creating new neurological pathways in your brain that allow your body to respond because you're constantly repeating words in a manner that increases your confidence.

When your confidence increases, the awareness of your abilities change. You create the self-fulfilling prophecy of your thoughts by looking for ways to validate your affirmations.

You use your senses by seeing the statements, hearing the statements, feeling and visualizing these statements AS IF they've always been a part of you. Again, they're statements about who you are, NOT who you want to become.

You "trick" your brain in a way that creates a reality you choose to believe. The consequence is that you look for ways to act. By your work and actions, you obtain the results.

The statements you choose should be sincere and admirable. In our affirmations, we tell ourselves we already are a certain way, have all we want, or have become the person we desire to be.

The way I teach affirmations requires a specific organized pattern. You must decide what you want before you write these affirmations. That's the key.

When deciding what to focus on, I suggest the first step is to think about what your coach tells you over and over. What are your coaches trying to teach you? When you identify what you're hearing, but maybe not listening to, then you need to create some initial affirmations around those words. It's a simple and effective way to start.

Once you cover those things you're being told to change, then move on to the higher level of self-coaching with these questions:
1. What do I want to become?
2. How do I want to be better than I was yesterday?

Then, make an affirmation from the answers to those questions. Much of these affirmations in sports may also come from seeing what other athletes can do that you haven't accomplished yet.

Who are your gymnastic superheroes? Who makes you say to yourself, "Wow, someone actually did that? I wonder if I can do that? I think I'll try!" This is where affirmations take-off and the Brain Game gets real.

Here are the rules for creating an effective positive affirmation:

1. **Be Positive.** This seems intuitive; however, there are many who mistakenly include words like, "I am not going to...." Only positive words are allowed in these statements. Keep all negative words out.
2. **Be Present.** Start with "I AM." There are other ways to begin, but in general, this is the most powerful and easiest way to start. This is one of the keys to affirmations. They must be as if you already are that kind of

person, or performing that kind of skill. Choose empowering words, not weak words. Speak to yourself from a place of confidence and capability, not inferiority or fear.

3. **Be Specific.** If you want specific results, then tell yourself what those details are in your affirmations. Instead of "I Am Amazing," you must ask yourself, what you want to be amazing at. What is going to change for you because you're "amazing"?

Your affirmation might look like this: "I am incredibly efficient when I complete each assignment on beam. This allows me to work on more skills that I enjoy." Another example for a specific skill might look like this: "I am calm, elegant, and confident every time I perform my flawless aerial on beam in competitions."

Tell yourself this is what you do and see how it's done in your mind as you say it. You have a clear picture and it no longer seems overwhelming to actually perfectly perform this skill in a competition.

The Brain Game routine:

1. Write one to three affirmations. Only do a few so you stay consistent and focused.
2. Post them on your mirror or someplace where you'll see them daily.
3. Read and vocalize those affirmations at least 10 times daily.
4. When you say the words, be looking at yourself in a mirror. There's power in eye contact. Have you ever tried talking with someone who avoids eye contact? It's crystal clear that they're insecure. You must speak to yourself with your eyes wide open and a connection with yourself! You must believe the new words you speak! This is what I call the "Mirror You," which is synonymous with the Real You!
5. Mirror You:
   a. Look at your eyes in the mirror.
   b. Say your affirmations out loud.

c. While you speak, use your visualization skills and feel the truth of the words in your heart!

6. Mind and Heart:

This is an addition that I haven't found in any of the training that I've had. You must include your mind and heart. Saying words has no impact without the emotion of belief and visual connection. Watch in your mind where you see yourself BEING and who you tell yourself YOU ARE.

Sometimes, we have cognitive dissonance occurring inside our minds. This is a psychology term where our values are not in line with our actions. We weigh what we want with what we are actually doing. This creates an unsettling mental state.

Cognitive dissonance, at times, reveals itself in the form of self-talk. When you want a change intensely enough, despite the automatic pilot your brain wants to offer you for action, you find yourself thinking words of encouragement and debate at the same time. You may even surprise yourself by vocalizing this debate aloud.

However, this self-talk isn't surprising to athletes. If you stand close to an elite-level gymnast, especially during high-performance moments, you may hear phrases voiced out loud. Elite-level athletes use words to keep their mind focused on what's most important: what they want.

They are their own best cheerleader and best friend, or their own worst enemy. We begin to create a self-fulfilling prophecy. This is another psychological term that means we create our results by our choices, beliefs, and actions that fall in line with what we want. Our results are proven by our thoughts, and our thoughts direct our emotions, desires, and drive. It all works together to create our performance, score, or outcome.

I would often have a set mental routine made up of words before any competition. Most higher-level athletes have these verbal routines. They will vocalize words and phrases to themselves to keep any distractions out.

I teach my athletes they need to choose what they will and won't allow inside their minds. Fear of the unknown likes to present itself as a valid thought. You decide a change will be made. In doing so, your senses are heightened, you find yourself talking out loud to convince your mind that you can make the uncomfortable sacrifices required for the desired change.

Interestingly, our negative thoughts don't seem so ready to present themselves vocally. They do at times, but, in general, we vocalize the positive phrases and thoughts to block the negative thoughts from entering into the gateway of our minds.

The cheerleader inside your head starts to find a voice. When you become aware of your goals, the cheerleader jumps in to encourage your progress toward change. However, your negative thoughts want to prevail and derail you from your new goal. It's easier.

Avoiding any change and staying in your comfort zone is the easiest form of living. We do this by filling our time with things that keep our mind distracted from what we really want. Avoidance at gym may occur when you choose to stay on beam as long as possible because beam is fun and easy, instead of rushing over to the bars where you know you'll have to do strength and skills that are hard and scary.

You can say you want to be an elite gymnast, but your actions are leading you far from that reality. Another example is choosing to sit in splits with the weight on your arms instead of allowing the gravitational pull to release the muscles into a lower split. Or, collapsing after the assigned 20 push-ups at the end of workout instead of seeing what you're really capable of and performing an extra 5 pushups without anyone else knowing.

Keeping yourself at stations that are "fun" and resisting the skills and drills that are "hard" is a natural and normal part of being an athlete. However, pushing past those initial "fun" stages of gymnastics and moving toward the difficult levels is the only way to experience true freedom as a gymnast. Freedom, in this sense, is when you can make your body do almost any skill flawlessly and get to experience a sense of flight and defying gravity.

This level of gymnastics enjoyment only comes from intense discipline. Unless you face and acknowledge your weaknesses and strive to make them become strengths, you'll remain as a lower level gymnast indefinitely.

These "things" have also been termed: distractions, buffers, addictions, and old habits.

We don't want to feel anything when we fall victim to allowing old, non-progressive thoughts to enter our gates and pass the Mind Guard (see Chapter 4). Not feeling or avoiding is, again, easy. Pushing against the negative takes effort, refusing entrance to an amazing place of your mind. That's what causes the cognitive dissonance.

We feel uncomfortable and will continue to feel this until the old neurological pathways have been paved over and new grooves are deep and secure. You'll feel uncomfortable until your new thought patterns have become a "new norm" for your reactions. It's awesome to feel this way. Welcome it because it means good things are headed your way as you form new pathways.

So, speak your affirmations out loud, drown out the voice inside that tells you to be content with your life of stagnation. Remember that change is the only form of true greatness.

Repeating affirmations daily will create more effective habits toward personal greatness and increase confidence in the process. Telling yourself statements to transform your inadequate areas into powerful skills creates change. That comes one affirmation at a time.

Affirmations are constant reminders of who you are, what you want, why you want it, and what you're willing to do to obtain it in every area of your life.

〜

Chapter 2 Highlights

- Affirmations are statements repeated regularly out loud in order to increase your confidence and productivity.
- These sentences remind you of what you need to think, do, and feel to be the athlete you aspire to become.
- Reading these statements out loud daily will enhance the way your mind responds to your environment.
- Your brain will look for ways to make those statements become a reality in your life.
- The four rules to writing a powerful affirmation statement include:

    1. Make them positive.
    2. Make them present.
    3. Be specific.
    4. Include your mind and heart.

What's ahead in Chapter 3

You will learn the formula to solve every athletic problem. An easy acronym is provided to help you remember how you can choose your feelings and thoughts in any circumstance.

Chapter 2 Action Items

1. Write one to three affirmations.
2. Post your affirmations on your mirror and repeat them 10 times out loud daily for a month.
3. Say it, See it, Feel it, and Believe it (heart and mind) as if it has already happened and it is already who you are.

Journal:

1. Free write about what you want to change: a specific skill or emotional state during gym. Use ideas from coaches' corrections to help you decide what to change.

2. At the end of the month, write how affirmations have impacted your confidence.

3

The Formula

"Start each day reminding yourself:
It's a good day to have a GOOD
DAY."

—Laurie Hernandez

"Set your goals, follow your dreams,
listen to your heart, and don't let
anything stand in your way."

—Brandy Johnson

"What I do depends on how I feel
about what I know."

—Kristine Twiggs

CHAPTER 3 TOOLS:

The CTFAR Formula

Life Coach School Director, Brooke Castillo, ascertains that the model CTFAR is the way to solve any life problem, with the key letter being the "T".

(Permission was given by Brooke Castillo for this chapter and its content.)

CTFAR

C=Circumstances- Factual, without opinion- This part is out of your control.

Every situation is neutral.

(Our Circumstances Trigger Thoughts)

T=Thoughts- You will have many thoughts. Pick one you want to examine. We attach thoughts to our situation, which gives the circumstance meaning.

(Our Thoughts Create Our Feelings)

F=Feelings- What is the feeling this thought gives you- one word description.

"Feelings are just chemical vibrations inside our bodies."

—Jody Moore

(Our Feelings Fuel Our Actions)

A=Actions- What do you do or not do in a situation when you feel this way?

We act based on our thoughts and feelings.

(Our Actions Create Our Results)

R=Results- This is the result for your Action and proof for your Thought.

(This Is Your Current Reality)

The CTFAR Formula for an elite gymnast would look something like this:

C=The Olympics

T=Any of the positive affirmations talked about in Chapter 2, such as: "I am successful," "I am practicing well," "I have the best coaches for me," "I have all the resources I need to achieve this goal," "I am capable and I have everything going for me to achieve this goal."

F=Confident, Capable, Strong, Quick, Resilient, Successful, Grateful

A=Give 110% every day. Do my mental/physical/emotional routine daily, seek help continuously, take care of every aspect of my life to be my best at every workout.

R=Success. Thoughts and Results always prove each other.

Notice I didn't include *winning* the Olympics as the result. Many will write the Olympics and you most certainly can. I have been a certified USAG judge and can tell you that writing down Olympics is a result that *is not* always in your control. However, personal success *is* in your control. Dream big! Mentally prepare for failure, but always expect success.

Your circumstance may be Level 1 right now. Put whatever your current situation is in the first line and what you want to have happen in the last line. Sometimes it helps to work from the *'feeling'* line first. How do you want to feel right now as a gymnast? Tweek the *'action'* and *'thoughts'* to fit what you want your results to be.

Mykayla Skinner of Desert Lights Gymnastics and coached by Lisa Spini, my former coach, set her sights on the Olympics. Based on the traditional path leading to competing in the Olympics, she received the qualifying score and placed high enough at the Olympic Trials to be on the Olympic Team.

Instead, she was chosen as an alternate for political reasons, of which I make no judgment.

This is just an example of that result, though. If she wasn't mentally tough and had written the Olympics as her end goal, she could have been devastated by her results.

Mykayla, and her coach could have chosen to be offended and not gone as an alternative to the Olympic Team. Instead of resentment, they prepared for Mykayla's role on that team and supported those who did compete.

She is currently a thriving gymnast for the University of Utah women's gymnastics team. I love Mykayla's example of enjoying the process rather than the circumstance. Her success comes from her positive thoughts about who she is, what her purpose is, what she is capable of doing, and whom she wants to serve in the process.

Lisa Spini agreed, stating, "We decided together that if [Mykayla] was going to be the Olympic alternate, that she would be the best alternate ever and that we would make it a positive experience, and we did. We had to do the same practice assignments every day as the gymnasts who got to compete and MyKayla did one great routine after another, never complaining, even though she knew that she probably wasn't going to get to compete." They were both mentally prepared for disappointment, but always expected success throughout their road to the Olympics.

Stanford Women's Gymnastics Team provided many opportunities to talk with professionals individually, and as a team, that increased my mental strength in order to maximize my performances. Between weight trainers, nutritionists, massage therapists, medical doctors, and sports psychologists, I was made aware and given plenty of information to help me to reach my goals.

There are many formulas and routines that have been created to provide great results. However, as a former collegiate gymnast who has worked with a variety of experts, I can now say that most of the ideas offered came down to very few foundational concepts.

One of these foundational elements is the fact that confidence in myself comes from my own thoughts. The fact that thoughts are the foundation of every action is an undeniable reality that has been restated by many other professionals for years.

If we considered our true end goal like a planned vacation, we would see that if we were only worried or excited about the final destination, then we would never leave home. Home is often our ultimate destination. What I mean is that when we plan a trip, we save, anxiously wait, research excursions, and look forward to reaching a predetermined place.

But in the end, what we really want most out of our travels is to return home safely. Thus, if we only want to return home, then why would be ever leave home in the first place? We leave out of a hope for enjoyed experiences and memories on our way there and back.

We not only find joy in the destination, but hope to find joy in the excursion as well. We must choose joy in the entire process of the planning, preparing, traveling, and returning. This is just a choice and change of perspective.

Gymnastics is a very short season in anyone's life. It's a demanding sport physically, emotionally, financially, and requires much time. Enjoying every aspect of your gymnastics career will create a deep and rich experience.

Changing your thoughts, as a gymnast, about your everyday gymnastic moments is entirely up to you and can simply be done by changing your thoughts about your situation right now. We are a product of our thoughts. As the epigraph above says, "Change your thoughts, change your world."

It's as simple as that, since our thoughts are the only things we can truly change anyway.

Changing thoughts is the catalyst that jump-starts a lasting change for our present and future.

Chapter 3 Highlights

- CTFAR method is the most succinct formula for concrete change in any athlete.
- CTFAR teaches that your thoughts are the key to solving any problem.
- Your thoughts always prove your results.
- Every part of the formula interacts seamlessly with each other.
- The acronym stands for:

  Circumstance

  Thoughts

  Feelings

  Action

  Results

What's ahead in Chapter 4

Find out what Cue Words and The Mind Guard are and how they will keep your mind tight and focused during every workout and especially in competitions.

Chapter 3 Action Item

Journal:

Use the CTFAR method every time you wish to feel differently about your athletic experience as well as make a lasting change in your career as a gymnast.

4

Mind Guard

"Focus: A process of diverting one's scattered forces into one powerful channel."

—Unknown

"My attitude is that if you push me toward something that you think is a weakness, then I will turn that perceived weakness into a strength."

—Michael Jordan

"Starve your distractions and feed your focus ."

—Amy Rees Anderson

CHAPTER 4 TOOLS:

Cue Word

A word that you choose to tell yourself in order to bring your thoughts in line with what you truly want.

Mind Guard

The idea that you place a figurative mental guard at the "gate" to your brain in order to filter your thoughts.

What do you desire? This is the goal-setting scenario and the "why" of everything we do. Walking into a gym on any given day, I can recall asking myself, "What do I want to do today?" Any elite athlete knows what they desire to achieve.

At every workout and every competition, they want their own personal standard of perfection.

Our minds can only focus on one thing at a time. You'll have many thoughts occurring, but you can only truly be focused on one at a time.

Your Mind Guard is a mental idea in which you place a guard at the entrance of your mind to filter which thoughts will be allowed to enter. The Mind Guard will work to keep all other irrelevant words and thoughts from entering or staying in your mental space.

I like to imagine my Mind Guard appearing as a guard at Buckingham Palace with the red uniforms, tall black hats, and long guns. Your thought must confront the Mind Guard before it is allowed entrance into an intensely respected place, a sacred place!

Imagine this guard at the gate of your mind deciding which thoughts are or are not welcomed and for how long they get to visit or reside. Signs such as "No entrance," "Don't enter," and "No soliciting" surround the outskirts.

The more your mind chooses to accept thoughts of change, the more resistance you'll feel from old thoughts. Your old thoughts will boycott your attempts at change. Your brain is wired to default to a type of cruise control of comfort and safety. The Mind Guard is constant, focused, and determined to provide your mind with the most protection possible, warding off intruding enemy-type thoughts.

Higher brain functioning is required to keep the Mind Guard active. You see this occur before a gymnast goes on an event in a meet when they are focused on just their physical and mental cues to produce their optimal performance level.

Some may think a gymnast is twitching or convulsing or has some problem, but what the gymnast is doing right before a difficult skill or routine, is performing the routine stationary in their mind or without actually physically performing.

Gary Mack, a sports psychologist, taught a similar technique when he worked with the Chicago Cubs that he termed a "Mental Locker" in his book, *The Mind Gym* (p. 138). When a player was preparing for an important event, he would tell him to deliberately take out of his mind "a problem or a personal concern," anything that would distract him from his focus as he changed from his day clothes to his game clothes. "By the time he had changed...he had shed all his distractions and personal concerns and was focusing on the present." (p. 138)

Gary goes on to say, "One key to achieving success in sports is learning how to focus on the task and not letting negative thoughts intrude. The mind can only concentrate on one thing at a time. I ask them to create a word that, when said to themselves, will block out all negative thoughts and help relieve tension."

Actions follow our thoughts and images. Don't look where you don't want to go. This is the goal of cue words and the Mind Guard.

Athletes try to place themselves, mentally, in a competitive situation so they can practice for an actual event coming up. An assistant collegiate coach told me that his baseball team was once asked to go into the women's gymnastics practice and be as distracting as possible. The gymnasts would perform a routine while the baseball team yelled, taunted, and tried to distract each gymnast from her routine.

As much fun as this sounds, the underlying purpose was crucial. This would help the women's gymnastics team prepare for an actual competition mentally. Athletes want to know how to keep a vigilant command on their mind, especially during a competition.

You need to experience what it will be like when you take your skills into an arena that is outside your comfort zone. You know what your gym feels like, sounds like, and creates for you. However, going to an opposing team's school and hearing the audience cheering so loudly that you cannot hear your own floor music is a completely different experience. If you're not mentally prepared, then doubts and distractions will make a typically flawless routine appear sub-par.

When I'm in a gym, I often have moms come to me and say, "My daughter can do her routines so well here at gym, but when she competes, she falls apart." This is typical. It's simply an untrained mind. You must practice environmental changes to your daily routine in order to truly understand yourself in every situation.

I love to coach beam. I love the mental games gymnasts go through on the beam. I love talking a gymnast through what their mind is doing when working on a specific skill, especially one that they feel particularly nervous executing.

Usually they have no idea what their mind is telling them; they only know how they feel, that their hands are sweaty, their heart is racing, or their stomach is doing flips. Once an athlete can decide what they truly desire, then I have them think of one or two words that summarize this desire.

In gymnastics, we call this your *"Cue Word."* I was taught to use this cue word technique when I was about 16 years old by a sports psychologist in Arizona. I have the gymnast tell me something that seems to work whenever they stick a specific skill. They may have to try many words, but we come up with a one-to-two-word phrase that they tell me out loud. As soon as they say the word out loud, they prep and go.

The gymnast will practice this for every move of their routine so that their body responds in a desired manner and eventually on automatic. They will vocalize a command and their body will perform consistently. Often, a cue word may stop working.

This is because the gymnast got stronger, faster, or more confident, so their rhythm changed. Once this happens, they just need to change their cue words. During the dance sections of routines, they may use a song or number rhythm to keep their mind tight. A 'tight mind' is a phrase used often in gymnastics and many other sports, which just means to keep their thoughts focused on the task at hand.

Cue words keep distractions out and build confidence in an athlete easier and faster than just doing another skill. Repetition is great, but if an athlete performs differently in meets than in the gym, or if they balk because of a "monkey mind" or mind distractions, then using a cue word for every step of a routine seems to work well.

First, the athlete must complete a skill consistently on a level they can manage mentally.

The athlete decides on a word that is helping to create that consistency. The only difference between the floor beam and a regulation height beam is four feet. The only difference for a gymnast between the floor beam and a regulation height beam is their thoughts.

If a gymnast can perform a series on a floor beam consistently, then that gymnast is capable of performing the same series the same way four feet off the floor on the same beam with the same consistency.

I recall one gymnast who would not go for her back walkover on the high beam. I told her to think of a word when she did them on the medium beam. She could perform them perfectly on a beam just a foot lower than the high beam over and over with no problem. The height would throw off her mental game.

When she was on the medium beam, she said, "Rainbow." So, we went with that. Every time she did a back walkover, she would vocalize the word *rainbow,* until it became part of that skill. When she got up to the high beam, she would hesitate. I asked her what she was thinking, and she said she didn't know.

Many gymnasts are perfectionists yet don't know exactly why their body isn't responding the way they would like it to respond. I asked if she felt nervous, if her palms were starting to sweat, if she thought of the word *rainbow.* She looked at me.

She knew what I was saying. She wasn't focused on what worked consistently for her. Instead, she was only focused on the fact that she was higher off the ground. Worry appeared. Fearful thoughts came to mind of things that might happen, even though those events had never occurred and may never occur.

She went back to the lower beam, then as soon as she was on the high beam, she vocalized,

"Rainbow" and went and stuck it. That skill was no longer a problem for her. She was able to keep her mind focused on the cue word only and not the external factors. This cue word worked well. This athlete rarely fell on that specific skill again.

Once a cue word is established and vocalized every time before the gymnast performs the skill, then you move up a level. For example, the gymnast goes to a higher beam. If she states the cue word and performs that skill well, then they are ready to try a higher level. If not, they must go back to the mentally capable level and continue working to find a word that tells their brain that their body can and will do something.

They need to create a new neural pathway for their mind to focus on instead of the habitual former one. This takes time and practice. It takes a while to cover an old neurological pathway and create a whole new pathway in the mind!

Patience is key here. Eventually, the gymnast will have a mental cue word routine and their body will respond without having to vocalize the cues. When affirmations, cue words, and visualization become a daily part of an athlete's life, then desired results occur at a much quicker pace.

Today, I use cue words to bring my mind into a place that I visit almost every night during a visualization and relaxation drill (these tools are discussed in *Flippin' Awesome Book Vol. II*). I say the cue words to lower my heart rate, empty my mind, and make me aware of the present.

The goals for my cue words serve a purpose just as they did when I used them in my athletic years. The more I say my cue words, the more I believe Ralph Waldo Emerson's quote, "Once you make a decision, the universe conspires to make it happen." Your mind responds to what you allow to enter into it.

The Mind Guard is at work. If you remain focused on the positive and seek motivational thoughts, then they will become your own reality. You can find your own cue words by answering the question, "What do I desire?"

If you answer this question, then you'll get to your deepest desire. Your desire drives your actions. If you desire something enough, you'll sacrifice nonessentials and focus on habits that may seem incredible to spectators. These new habits will bring you a sense of direction and success. If you know what you desire, then you know what you're willing to do to achieve that objective.

In his book, *Start with Why,* Simon Sinek suggests you find your "why" for what you want by working from the inside out in order to achieve lasting and great results. Your motivation comes from inside. Peel back layers by asking yourself WHY you want what you say you want. You continue to ask, "Why?" until you reach a feeling.

If you've done enough work on yourself, then, eventually, your why will be "because of love." Love for yourself and others. This is when you know that what you want is meaningful and lasting. You now have a reason for keeping a tight range on your choices. And you now have a cue word to remind you of that reason.

Thus, a cue word is a word to bring your mind back to what you want. If you don't know what you want, then cue words have no purpose. Just like in Lewis Carroll's, *Alice in Wonderland,* "If you don't know where you are going, it doesn't matter which path you choose."

Once you know what you want, and peel down the layers to the reason being from love and capabilities, then you'll find a word to remind you of your purpose for gymnastics. Your Mind Guard will stand on active duty to filter nonconforming words and thoughts.

I used cue words for years of competitive gymnastics in every move of every routine to prep my mind to focus on what would provide the most success. I use cue words when I work with athletes today at the gym or during mental training sessions. This helps them push out all distractions that keep them from what they desire.

Use cue words whenever you find your mind wandering off the pre-planned path to success and into areas of self-destruction.

Chapter 4 Highlights

- Cue words are predetermined words to remind you of what you desire and why.

- Use cue words when your focus begins to self-destruct due to distractions.

- The Mind Guard acts as a mental guard to keep all nonconforming words out of your brain.

- Using these methods will keep you persistent and diligently working toward achieving your athletic dreams.

What's ahead in Chapter 5

Find out how to reignite the flame and keep your passion for gymnastics alive through creating your own symbolic "Red Book."

Chapter 4 Action Items

Journal:

1. Answer the following questions in a "free write" in your journal:

   (Free Write means to write for a set amount of time without stopping or thinking about your response.)

   What do I desire? (Do a free write often to this question.)

   Why do I desire it?

   What is one word that reminds me of what I desire and why?

2. Keep your cue word near you on a paper, on your mirror, and in your morning affirmations.

3. Use your Mind Guard to filter out other words or self-talk that do not agree with your cue word and its meaning.

5

Red Book

"Each of us has a fire in our hearts for something. It's our goal in life to find it and keep it lit."

—Mary Lou Retton

"There is always going to be a reason why you can't do something; your job is to constantly look for the reasons why you can achieve your dreams."

—Shannon Miller

"There is power in people who dream big and who try hard."

—Harold Klemp

CHAPTER 5 TOOLS

The Red Book:

The internal incentive that keeps you moving. Something within that excites you to action. A symbolic gymnastics optional "Red Book" is filled with all the reasons you look forward to going to the gym every day.

Years ago, I went to the hospital after I broke and dislocated my middle finger during a vault attempt into the foam pit. My dad and doctor wouldn't listen to me as I insistently told them both, "It's okay; it's not broken. Can we get back to gym now?" I recall the doctor stating it was broken and dislocated.

So, then my only question was, "Will it make my finger worse if I still do bars?" Bars was the hardest event for me to keep up strength and I was just learning some exciting new skills. I had no desire to take a break. Unfortunately, I did have to wait a few weeks to get back to swinging on the bars, but I learned a great lesson from this experience.

My middle finger was broken because of the way I pulled my tuck for the front handspring on vault. This vault is a forward-facing skill where the gymnast runs down the runway, jumps onto a springboard, flies forward over the vault table, and completes a forward flip in a ball-like position before landing on the mat. I never pulled the front tuck that way again.

And I also learned to stick my handspring fronts more easily because of the new technique I learned to use as I grabbed my shins for the tuck. I was always willing to keep moving forward toward my athletic goals.

Later, I hyperextended both of my elbows and had to keep ice packs on my elbows all day at school for a couple weeks. This happened because I missed a release move on bars, and instead of landing properly on the floor, I reached for the ground.

This was in warm-ups for a competition. The doctors were surprised that neither of my elbows had broken. I was supposed to do a different bar release, but my mental monkeys (discussed in an earlier chapter) came to play in my head that day, so I switched, last minute, to an old release.

I hadn't prepared properly for this last-minute bar routine change. Again, I learned some valuable lessons. I learned very quickly to land flat on my stomach and never reached for the ground again. I also learned to keep performing what I practiced in the gym. Personal, unplanned, and last-minute changes aren't wise.

From these two experiences, I could not use one hand nor bend my arms for an extended period. However, that didn't mean my legs didn't work.

There was still so much to do in the gym with my legs.

Physical ailments would not hold me back from moving forward in the sport. My inner-drive for progress as a gymnast would never rest. I had so much to learn from watching others, or perfecting what the rest of my body could do while my broken parts healed.

This is a personality trait that is impossible to implant into another person. It's the drive that comes from a passion burning inside to see how far you can go. It's an inner mission that comes from the soul and decides every thought and choice.

In the book, *Jonathan Livingston Seagull,* by Richard Bach, a seagull recognizes that his passion for flying reaches far outside the basic needs of life, but rather for the enjoyment of life.

He tries to teach others how to enjoy flying in the same manner as he does, only to realize that there are very few who care to do so. In fact, only one other seagull truly tried to hear the message Jonathan was trying to share. It was discouraging to Jonathan.

This is the difficult part of explaining what it's like to enjoy something in life so much that it's just part of your soul. You're not you without this part of you. Unless you have found something that's as much a part of you as breathing, then you may not feel like you can relate to this concept yet, but through utilizing the ideas in this book, that connection could be a reality for you as well.

Creating that kind of passion in another person cannot come from anywhere but inside. In the end, we all act and think for ourselves. We find fulfillment in the boundaries that we place on our own lives. No one can choose passions for us..

Motivation and passion are inseparable. It's interesting to me when I see raw talent and want to develop a child's skill level, only to find that the natural talent will never be realized in that specific area because the child has no motivation or passion for gymnastics. Motivation is one of those gifts that are hard to develop. It comes from within.

Either you want to work hard for something and see where you can go, or you don't. *Motivation comes from knowing what you want and why you want it.* If a child is given a gift in one area of their life, and everyone around them sees this talent and are excited about the child's gift, it really means nothing if the child doesn't see or enjoy the gift.

You can try to force a child into a sport they don't love but are good at. However, rarely will the child go far. Parents will wonder what more they could have done. You cannot give a person "drive" if there's nothing inside to drive. Without the desire to continually do your best during any circumstance, as an athlete, you'll eventually find new interests.

I competed with a former teammate who didn't love gymnastics. However, she recognized her talent and worked to receive a full-ride scholarship. I was informed that once those years of gymnastics were over, she never stepped foot in a gym again. She knew what she wanted and worked through years of a sport for a goal that was worth it to her.

It's surprising and unimaginable to my mind to have spent so much time and effort toward a goal with no passion along the way. However, elite athletes are able to drop the unimportant things or things others would consider essential in order to obtain a future goal. This requires a very mature mentality to persist in that effort for such an extended time.

When I was leaving for college, my dad advised me to "pray hard, work hard, and play hard." This was something I wrote down and taped to my desk all four years of college. It was a reminder of a balanced life for my personality type.

He's also the one who suggested I read the book, *Jonathan Livingston Seagull*. I didn't read it until years later, but once I did, I immediately realized why it was a good suggestion and how much it resonated with who I was. I, like Jonathan, learned that my talent was also my passion. I wanted to "fly." I assumed everyone else in the gym wanted this as well.

I recently judged an inner-squad competition at a gym where a former club teammate of mine, Meagan (Wright) Tabla runs the girls' team program. We sat talking about the gymnasts and her daughter specifically. She mentioned that her daughter doesn't have the "fight to win" in her.

I informed Meagan that I rarely had that fight to win. She turned to me inquisitively and asked "Then what kept you going?" That was easy! I loved finding out what the assignment was from Lisa Spini, our head coach, so I could complete the assignment with perfection (to mine and my coaches' standards) and then.... open **The Red Book.**

I loved both the feeling of performing a routine perfectly AND discovering what more my body was capable of doing. My teammate had no idea what I was talking about. I had to remind her that all the optional skills were (and still are) listed in a red book.

The Red Book was a huge, red, hardbound three-ring binder full of every skill that had been performed, divided into each event by colored tabs. Every page included simple descriptions and pictures, along with the judges' shorthand and an individual number attached to each skill. The pages were arranged in a progressively harder skill difficulty level. There was just one Red Book at the gym. Thus, we had to share and, eventually, the pages became rather worn.

When I became a judge and bought my own Red Book for the first time, I wondered why I hadn't bought myself one years earlier. I spent so much time looking at new skills I could try and combinations I could do. That was one of my greatest motivators.

I just wanted to experience another skill. I worked hard daily at the gym in order to be able to flip open that Red Book and imagine myself trying out the many options. "Which one did I want to try today?"

With my body currently unable to perform those skills physically anymore, I feel I'm not deprived at all, since my mind recalls precisely how every skill felt through years of visualization (a tool taught in *Flippin' Awesome Gymnast Vol. II*). When I want to "be" a gymnast now, all I do is sit still for a second and I enjoy those skills over and over in my head.

My body responds in little movements as to the twists and flips and details required to perform any skill. My default or "bored" mind typically goes straight to bars: Giant full geinger shoot-over. A bar combination moving from the high bar to low bar.

I am and will always be a gymnast performing 10.0 routines mentally. Nevertheless, it feels amazing and real, just as it did in my deja vu moment when I was 16 at the Delta Center (discussed in My Story). The experience had me asking myself, "Am I asleep in my bed or actually performing?"

It doesn't matter; it's all the same. I can even perform any new skill I see on television today. I still have to work mentally at adjusting timing and tightness in order to perfect each skill. I imagine exactly when I would twist or flip, and the timing or rhythm of the skill.

I still do gymnastics. Just not physically. It will always be one of my favorite hobbies. I *prayed hard* for safety and help to progress. I *worked hard* to complete the assigned tasks. I *played hard* every time I got to open that RED BOOK!

Dr. Robert Sapolsky is a neuroendocrinologist who teaches biology and neurological sciences at Stanford. He has researched the function of dopamine and how it affects our actions. Through his studies, he has found that dopamine (which is the pleasure chemical in our bodies) doesn't come *after* we perform, as formerly thought.

Once we get in a regular routine, dopamine is released before we even get started with a project. This finding was fascinating and made sense. Just waking up in the morning made me excited to get to gym. I didn't have to wait to be doing gymnastics to have the "pleasure chemical" released in my body.

I still don't need the actual performance of any gymnastics for me to feel the "dopamine hit" now. I feel my heart race, my shoulders tighten, my stomach flutter, and my hands get sweaty when I visualize being on the beam about to execute a series.

Dr. Sapolsky suggests it's the anticipation of an event and not the actual event that gives us the chemical release of dopamine. And that's correct for any true gymnast's experience as well.

A gymnast will wake to thoughts of being in the gym, spend the day thinking about or physically trying to find space to practice one more handstand, and end their day dreaming about how their practice went or will go tomorrow.

If you're seeking an Elite-level of gymnastics, you must find the symbolic "red book" that will inspire you to reach beyond your own knowledge. You must seek for something bigger and desire something harder and greater than your current abilities.

This will provide the continual dopamine chemicals to be released inside you, which, in turn, will give you a greater desire for more enjoyment in your sport. It's a cyclical pattern of excitement toward success.

Chapter 5 Highlights

- The Red Book is literally a book full of every gymnastics skill performed and given a value in the sport of gymnastics.

- This book was a place for me to retire to, after every completed assignment, for inspiration and elation.

- Your Red Book is your own symbolic force that moves you toward reaching for and trying something new.

- It can be the actual gymnastics optional book, a vision board, a promise to yourself, or even a team goal.

- This "carrot dangling in front of your face"-type object will create excitement from within your soul.

- As you discover your own "Red Book," you'll continually long to progress and unveil your athletic potential as it drives your passion daily.

What's Ahead in Chapter Worksheets

As you implement the chapter tools incorporated into these worksheets, you'll discover more energy, desire, and commitment to yourself as a gymnast. Your purpose will become clear and almost tangible. See how to take the methods discussed and put them into action by completing the worksheets provided.

Chapter 5 Action Items

Challenge:

1. What is your symbolic "Red Book" as a gymnast?

2. What pulls you toward the gym and makes you want to crush fears and take action in your daily workouts?

Journal:

1. Keep a journal of your emotional ups and downs from your daily workouts.

2. Write anything that inspires, drives, and excites you about gymnastics.

3. Look for patterns in your journal entries. When energy is low, where are you looking for the passion to come from? Do you have an external or internal reason for participating in gymnastics.

APPENDIX I

CHAPTER WORKSHEETS

Chapter 1: Blast Off Sequence Worksheet

Challenge: 3-2-1 Go!

1. Start each morning by getting yourself out of bed with the "3-2-1 Go!" rule, then see how often you can apply it throughout your workouts. Write about your experience using this tool:

_____

_____

_____

_____

_____

_____

_____

_____

_____

_____

Journal:

1. Write down one moment where the you made yourself do something that you would typically choose not to do because you responded to an idea and told yourself "3-2-1 Go!" before you let you mind persuade you otherwise. If you hesitated to take action, then take time to write down why. Was there really a good reason to hesitate? What might have happened if you had not hesitated? What's the worst-case scenario? What's the best-case scenario? What might happen in the future if you choose to just go and do, instead of stop and consider? And, of course, wisdom should always prevail in answering personal questions.

Today I chose to use the 3-2-1 Go! Tool when I:

_____

_____

_____

_____

_____

_____

Today I hesitated to take action because:

_____

_____

_____

_____

_____

_____

CHAPTER 2: Brain Game Worksheet

The Brain Game:

1. Write one to three affirmations. Rules: Present Tense, Positive, and Specific

   a. Example: <u>I am</u> <u>calm, confident, and patient</u> <u>when I perform (certain skill).</u>

   b. _____

   _____

   c. _____

   _____

   d. _____

   _____

2. Read and vocalize your affirmations at least 10 times every morning while looking in the mirror.

3. Say it, See it, Feel it, and Believe it (heart and mind) as if it has already happened.

CHAPTER 3: The Formula Worksheet

Fill out the following lines of the CTFAR Formula

1. Current Situation:

Circumstance:_____

Thought:_____

Feelings:_____

Action:_____

Result:_____

2. Ideal Situation:

Circumstance:_____

Thought:_____

Feelings:_____

Action:_____

Result:_____

Chapter 4: Mind Guard Worksheet

Journal:

1. What is your cue word?

   _____

   _____

   _____

   _____

2. What if **Love** were your cue word for gymnastics and as a gymnast? What might be different for you as a gymnast?

   _____

   _____

   _____

   _____

3. Today I kept my Mind Guard up when I:

   _____

   _____

   _____

   _____

Chapter 5: The Red Book Worksheet

Challenge:

1. Find your own symbolic "Red Book." What do you look forward to as a gymnast?

Journal:

1. Write anything that inspires and excites you about gymnastics.
2. Today I learned:

_____

_____

_____

_____

_____

_____

_____

_____

APPENDIX II

STRONG MIND WORKSHEET

1. What do you want to change? What do you most desire?

_____

_____

2. What are you telling yourself about your possible change? What problems arise when you think about making a change?

_____

_____

3. At the front of every problem, write the word, OPPORTUNITY.

_____

_____

4. Post the quote: "What I tell myself is ten times more powerful than what anyone else is telling me." (author unknown)

_____

_____

5. How do you want to feel right now?

_____

_____

6. What will you do to get that feeling?

_____

_____

7. Write two affirmations about the change you plan to make. Remember to post and say them out loud 10 times daily while looking in your eyes in the mirror.

_____

_____

Rules: Present Tense, Positive, Specific, Heart and Mind

    a. _____

    b. _____

CONGRATULATIONS AND THANK YOU FOR READING THIS BOOK, WORKING TO CRUSH YOUR FEARS & INCREASE YOUR CONFIDENCE!

About the Author

Amy Twiggs is a wife and a mother of four teenagers. She is a former elite gymnast and, in 1995, she was a member of the developmental National Women's Gymnastics Team. She received a full-ride athletic scholarship for gymnastics from Stanford University where she obtained a Bachelor's Degree in Psychology with a focus in Health & Development. Mental Training is her passion. Amy's education has provided many opportunities for her to give back to athletes.

She has coached and choreographed for 25 years at a variety of gymnastics facilities. She is a former USAG Judge and currently owns the Flippin' Awesome Gymnastics facility in St. George, Utah.

~

If you are interested in contacting Amy Twiggs please email her at

flippinawesomecoaching@gmail.com

Made in the USA
Middletown, DE
20 February 2020